Shearsman

93 & 94

Winter 2012 / 2013

Edited by
Tony Frazer

GW00724574

Shearsman magazine is published in the United Kingdom by
Shearsman Books Ltd
50 Westons Hill Drive, Emersons Green, BRISTOL BS16 7DF

Registered office: 30-31 St James Place, Mangotsfield, Bristol BS16 9JB
(this address not for correspondence)

www. shearsman.com

ISBN 978-1-84861-230-3
ISSN 0260-8049

We are grateful to Mercure de France, Paris, for permission to print in this issue
translations of three poems by Yves Bonnefoy: 'Ici, toujours ici' from
Hier régnant désert (1958), & "Prestige, disais-tu de notre lampe et
de feuillages…" and 'L'arbre, la lampe' from *Pierre écrite* (1965).

John Mateer's poem 'The Copts' has previously appeared, together with a German
translation, in *Das Magazin der Kulturstiftung des Bundes*. Alice Miller's poem
'After Battle' has previously appeared in *Landfall*.

Subscriptions and single copies:
Current subscriptions—covering two double-issues, each around 108 pages, cost
£13 in the UK, £16 for the rest of Europe (including the Republic of Ireland), and
£18 for the rest of the world. Longer subscriptions may be had for a proportionately
higher payment, which insulates purchasers from further price-rises during the
term of the subscription. North American customers may find that buying single
copies from online retailers in the USA will be cheaper than subscribing. £18
equates to about $28 at the time we went to press. The reason for this is that
subscriber copies are sent by mail and UK postage rates have risen significantly.

Back issues from nº 63 onwards (uniform with this issue)—cost £8.50/$13.50
through retail outlets. Single copies can be ordered for £8.50, post-free, direct from
the press, through the Shearsman online store, or from bookstores in the UK and
the USA. Earlier issues, from 1 to 62, may be had for £3 each, direct from the press,
where they are still available, but contact us for prices for a full, or partial, run.

Submissions
Shearsman operates a submissions-window system, whereby submissions are only
accepted during the months of March and September, when selections are
made for the October and April issues, respectively. Submissions may be sent
by mail or email, but email attachments—other than PDFs—are not accepted.
We aim to respond within 2–3 months of the window's closure.

CONTENTS

Mary Leader	4
Robert Saxton	7
Mark Goodwin	11
Julie Maclean	16
Geraldine Clarkson	19
G.C. Waldrep	22
Susie Campbell	26
Ray DiPalma	28
Simon Smith	32
Alice Miller	38
James McLaughlin	40
Cristina Viti	43
Sharon Morris	47
Harry Guest	49
Linda Black	54
Edward Mackay	57
Claire Crowther	59
John Mateer	61
Mark Dickinson	64
Keri Finlayson	68
Peter Robinson	72
Kate Ashton	75
Sean Reynolds	76
Lucy Hamilton	79
Charles Hadfield	82
Andrew Sclater	84
Ian Seed	87
Aidan Semmens	90
Corey Wakeling	94
Yves Bonnefoy	97
(translated by Ian Brinton & Michael Grant)	
José Kozer	99
(translated by Peter Boyle)	
Marina Tsvetaeva	103
(translated by Christopher Whyte)	
Biographical Notes	105

from **Crone Cards**

VI.

When in the night it rains, the opening
Elaborations of perception wear
The deeply hooded cloak of amnesia
But clearly, indeed pointedly, also
Memories too awful to bear in mind.
Open-mouthed privation. Clearly, indeed
Pointedly, the homed male arrives, the
Hidalgo with a radish to give her,
And days sunny, a kickshaw and a dress,
And fava beans as well. Of course she will
Bargain: *nunc pro tunc,* now for then, *quid pro
Quo,* this for that, tit for tat, how much and
Of what kind. Of course she has enough sense
To close her lantern when dashing in rain.

VII.

Reasoning she leaves to symbolism.
Crown surviving its oxidized braiding.
Anything that's like the hand in the ice,
Preserved by fluke. Whereas slumbering yields
Young occasions. Postcard from a sailor
Who moored a yacht in the crack-space between
Mirror and frame. Youth's connectivities
Once strengthened neurons. But yes she's darkness
And yes she limps. In one recent dream, twelve
Moons and three druidic philosophers
Pulled modem life through an exhibition
Of ash and eaten stone, cooled in a pool.
Peat. Now *there's* a crucial continuum:
Degrees of soft/hard, of how fast it burns.

4

VIII.

By Michaelmas the sun is not working
All that hard and not promising very
Much. It rises, grows round, can be thought of.
First freeze warning comes and goes. She just reads.
The essay 'Rotten Sun' gives her access
To the idea of Sun "or / as" Flower.
"Especially asters," she would add. Her
Muse, perhaps again with Zarathustra
Nearby, looks up with a guarded sadness,
Pale, powerless against memory. He
Once rode along the elevation of
Noon, cycling into brass shafts, drawn among,
Drawn out of, those shafts of brass light.
Work feels Sacrificial in autumn, and confused.

IX.

Hers is complementary to the myth
Of Icarus which, from the Cyrillic
Of Arkady, "is particularly
Expressive from this point of view; it splits
The sun in two: the one that was shining
At the moment of boy Icarus's
Elevation, and the one that melted
The wax causing failure and a screaming
Fall when Icarus got too close." The moon
Splits the sea in two: the one that stays calm
While negation prepares to wax to red;
The one that gets hysterical enough
To attack land, shag plants loose at the root,
Break: hill, stone, rubble, pebble, gravel, sand.

X.

And should she elevate mythology
Above history? What material
Differences are there? She favors motley.
Conjuress, bark-dust in her scales, woman
With eyes like foil kiln-melted, then crumpled,
Then frozen hard again. From strands she lures
Yams onward, unto form. She thinks she wants
Some old falcon with bark-dust in his hair.
What kind of society comes up with
Sumptuary laws? At any rate, she
Cannot afford fringe in colors shipped from
Other nation-states. She has only read
Cochineal, and much forbidden *woad.*
Peasant, she goes in scorched shades & shades bleached.

XI.

She sleeps alone. No. Beside her sleeps her
Pet. No one ever singularly sleeps.
Sleep is like a bead. Simultaneous
Sleep, however, does not mean that sleep is
Entirely unified. It's not. The
Asleep that is a specific asleep
Is always also a feather of one
Death or another whooshing solar-ward.
Except that sleeping is not synchronized
Together with or fully controlled by
One such sun. This is one fact which in turn
Links specific to general dawn, a
Blurring hare's day, all the runnings of, *we,*
Who wake or die in more than one system.

The Floating Village

Shore swindlers plot their pitch
on a far beach, landing their catch
of moonshine under an eye patch.

Those hills are a habitat of stars
too dim to give any cause
for panic's clash of oars.

Bare feet that never rocked
on yielding sand are circumspect,
on wood too personal to be wrecked.

Our evening's hymn is the nets
in the air, thrashing above cats
who swim—through shoals of gnats.

The possible thief's a spry,
strong breeze, just hearsay
at dawn, a sting of lake spray.

High on the lake's lap we sleep
on a raft of love, grief's isotope,
shy of all but the gentlest slope

and the flimsiest gate,
delicate within our moat,
no bell on the reed-thin goat.

The China Shop Pictures

There's evidence of contact in the glue—
untoward incident, intemperate phrase.
The gift shop's magic shield's a crackle-glaze.

The whiplash tail's the thing you want to watch,
mad python's thwack a shelf-length from the flitch.
Some willowy dream will crash—the question's which?

Cuff'im! Lasso the snout and staunch the riot,
rampage of drivelling culture in the gut.
It's a knocking-shop for an existential rut.

Muck in and grab the vandal's big brass ring.
Cossett the wounded king but cull the kong.
A headache's cool: a bellyache's all wrong.

If the geisha's haiku picnic goes ahead
as planned, in the meadow, unleash your healing word.
Insinuate the lamb in the thundering herd.

We're fools to think of cherry and pine as tame,
it's muscle that strings the gardener in his prime.
Wholeness is yesterday, the stench of time.

The moment's drunkenness is rocket fuel,
shrinking the manhood of the golden mile.
When will the herd parade in single file?

Only when Darwin learns to speak Chinese
and dragons emulate the geisha's poise,
hungry enough to swallow bestial noise.

Enamel's the coward's way, though it sells,
being safer in alleyways than porcelain bowls.
Smart sweethearts know you haven't paid in souls.

Awkwardly turning, caught in mid-air like a ball,
the lowliest bowl is now most mythical—
like the world-shaking, china-shattering bull.

Shutter Buddy Boogie

I'm a shutter buddy, and I always have been.
    I pride myself on my skills,
    both social and technical.
I've been shuttering since I was seventeen.
    I can do plain, I can do fancy frills.

I'm a shutter buddy, and I'm Captain Keen.
    The strong win merit, redeeming the demure.
    Anybody pregnant knows I'm on call—
I'll sweat for them, an affable machine
    to close the shutter, keeping their bairn secure.

I'm a shutter buddy, and I'll always wait
    for any lovely, ladylike mum-to-be
    whose in-tray's impossibly tall.
Keyholder, yes, but you can't pull down the gate.
    Don't worry, help's on hire, you're safe with me.

I'm a shutter buddy, and loth to accept a nightcap.
    A thankyou's brushed off with a graceful mumble.
    Inwardly I'm having a ball.
Sinewy and caring, I pump iron in the gap,
    slamming the grill with a flourish, rarely a stumble.

I'm a shutter buddy, with a midwife's understanding.
    Home birth, epidurals, baby names and scans—
    we're waxing lyrical,
while the lift cranks up, chatting on the landing.
    Outside I sign the bumps of pregnant fans.

I'm a shutter buddy, and my ballpoint's Zorro,
    a rapier dancing in the Hollywood hills.
    My autograph's quite valuable.
Same time, same place, same shutter groupies, tomorrow.
    I can do plain, I can do fancy frills.

Dungeness Rabbits

Though rabbits, ancestrally,
    have bought their freedom,
    many are born to the gravel-beds
    whose homesteads have herb gardens.
Herb gardeners complain, of course,
    yet sometimes might buy
    a flavoursome rabbit
    from the smokery, shot-free—
    because the smoke-master's boy
    aims accurately at the head
    on his evening walks,
    missing hours of telly.

Many homesteads are filled
    with the shifting blue light
    that tells of settlement, of family life—
    matters unspoken, unresolved.
There on the screen, the triumph
    of the unembarrassed.
Then the door makes a noise
    and in marches a drinker,
    or a power station worker,
    or the rabbit shooter with a bottle
    of single malt's worth of
    warm furry corpses.

Gleam-form at Resipole, December 2011

sudden cloud-slot slides

              inland up off

sea blue-black sky split

        by bright

sun clips

    hill-ridge fractures

           glow across

Loch Sun Art's pelt

      l i t r i p p l e s c o l l e c t

              otter-shape

long whisker

        -wake arrowing

from round snout now a

          gloss-otter's

tapered snake of tale slides

            gone cloudsclose

A Casteal Tioram, A Moidart, A December 2011

a we fade
in tuned by a time's pin

point we flickers of selves clad
in Gore-tex as
hail sizzles our figures a we imagine
men in wool drenched &
ferocious congealed in centuries

isthmus sand plants

                                        an us as
                                        fresh foot
                                        steps as

ragged battlements hang
on a gabbro uvula in a Loch
Moidart's mouth we cross

                              a thread of land we

approach a box of stone a
box of slots of light an
excrescence of human-animal endeavour a
weather-raped dying shelter a
defenceless hollow crag

yellow signs warn & command
do not enter a histories' crumb
ling fabrication(s) we

                              squeeze through prized

apart wire & find some
selves of us with
in a solid Escher-esque closet

algae-splodged & mossily-written-on
block walls drip as hail falls
from sky's printer all
that is 3d-touchable being

                                        built
                                        up in
                                        layers
                                        of un
                                        saids

despite some authority's
black-on-yellow wasp-sharp signs

                                        we find 9

white construction-site hardhats nuzzled
together like albino lady
birds on an

                                        altar
                                        &

aluminium ladders at
jaunty angles giving
access

to greazy battlements where count
less footfalls freeze-froze noise

some i of a Me climbs
up a snake-sm
ooth yet snake-int
ricate calendar on wet aluminium rungs some

shape paces
battlements as a distant
Eigg's jagged anvil flattens & anneals

tide's deep ditch-green fragrance gleams
on castle walls as a loch's pewter ripples
hail-hazed hills pebbles pines bladderwrack & oaks
miniaturise to a memory's brooch

all while white helmets huddle
bodiless: some council in
session as

a buried gauzy energy of their bones cools to begin

fade

Note: Casteal Tioram (pronounced 'chee-rum') is Gaelic for 'dry castle'.

Strontium & Gold, A December 2011

Strontian River's th
ick white cords wrig

gle & loop be
tween a glen's

he   athery wings
hill-f   og caps a

holl   ow-of-world
inno   cent of alchemy

now as if win   d had
torn a tr   ee-part

free & fl   ung
it through cl   oud a

dark broad bar soars

finger feath   ers gr   aze
wet air's vo

iceless noises some

lead-grey crea
ture-shape a

bout to be
gone pulls

gold to ground now

ea   gle claws fall
as cryst

all   isation
from sky's mine beak

punc   tures pelt sud
denly as if woun

ded   a loll
oping fea   thery

rock jerks
blood's bits

through grasses as

ele   ments repeat
edly f   lock &

scat

Note: Strontian is a river & a village in western Lochaber. In the 18th Century the hills to the north of the village were mined for lead. The element strontium was first isolated from the mineral strontianite, which was discovered in the mines.

JULIE MACLEAN

expresh vs. colonial landscape

he's too hot to touch   in bed after midnight
batteries chokked from the charge of the day

he's painted his years in the manner of von Guerard
monster canvas   little leaves   shady detail in his
felt-funny hat
           he's crag-man with scalpel   on the lookout
for the next big commish   big wheels spitting
rev rev revving   in three point perspective
           in a Baroquish frame

her days are broad-brushed in the sweep and
gloom of a Rothko   wall papery   covering cracks
the worry of a Tucker   fug of a Turner
           blinding hangover   too many men   cigarettes
in younger days Hester melancholic they say she had a wide aorta
           blood poured over her gunmetal carpet
turning it black   impatiens petals splatter
    white tiles   think American Beauty
           don't think Pro Hart

yet side by side
           at the end of each day
                     they say 'Had a good one?'
                          and watch Deal or no Deal
                                   before the Six o'clock News

Barest essentials for 19th Century explorers

European

A camel
A horse for jerking
A creek for tracing
A good deodorant
A flinty, quartzy desert for trudging across
The red white and blue in a rucksack
A tree to carve initials in
A prize
A prayer

Indigenous

An eye
Leather soles Made in Australia
A kangaroo banging across the horizon
A goanna skittering over a saltpan
A waterhole
The red, black, ochre in the marrow
A rock
A stick
A story

A nonnet for my first love, not a 'shall I compare thee...'

thank you mum for such a wonderful gift
a rugged Heathcliff beauty to love
except when I said 'No' to his coming inside
he put on a bull's red hide and horns and with
cloven hooves stuck firm in
the shag pile he humped the air
offering up to me
two marbled logs of
bloodless sperm in a
newborn's pale
veined caul
joined down the middle like the twins from Siam

with love and care I split the two
I took one for me and gave one to you

Down Among the Dead Birds
(Sick Bird Ode)

1. Coldblooded blackbird
electrified
frozen in red for a split second
before feathers spit and sizzle

2. Fried black bird
marinated in Tamara
with a nod to ginger and chocolate

3. Reformed robin
cut cute
into heart-shapes

4. Salty wren, round
and around the globe
in a boat

5. Humongous humming-bird
gastric ring vibrating
in the dead head
of a promiscuous foxglove

6. Craven raven
blenching

7. Daily nightingales
disturbing the piece

8. Difficult swallow
oesophagus clenching incredibly
impossibly

9. Crooked rook
two up, two down
and one across

10. Whore-hawk
her eye on the humming
bird

11. Limping swift
sore thumb

12. Two-a-penny sparrow
hanging its costly dead
head

13. A grudge dredged
from an oily slick
by a budgerigar-

heron. Her on guard dowdy at the nest
while the emerald-jet male pulls
worms, a frog,
to general applause

14. Blind eagle
hawk-eyed.
Her desire running after the man.
Ave. Ave.

Under Bougainvillea, in Full View of the Stars
(*After Hours*)

A mis-spent life is brilliant
for luring the Muse.
You wait for her in the dark,
batter down passion
with a club, knuckle–dust fear
into the cellar. Take pride
in your threshold of boredom
which one day you hope
to carry her across.

At the door of a party
you let gales of brash sweaty air
wash over you as you stand
baffling your gaze. Brazen out
barrowfuls of abuse
which they wheel to the bins.
The stink. You touch her arm.
No words. It might take
decades of holding your breath
to get a whisper. Dozens of

A mis-meant life isn't valiant,
flooring the Muse.
I waited for her in the dark
battering passion
with a club. Took pride
in polishing my threshold
of boredom, which one day
I hoped to carry her across.

I let draughts of brackish air
tickle me as I stood at the door
of a factory, packing and
repacking my gaze. Flinched
at fish fins in the sluice.
More drink. I gripped her arm.
No words. It could take
a martyrology

of mini–deaths to kick–start a
voice, ginger stretching of shins,
to pump up a syllable.

A miscreant life is resilient,
curing the Muse.
Waiting with her in the dark,
better than passion
at a club. Taking pride
in flesh held in her
bedroom, her skill
at amateur lacrosse.

At the door of a villa,
bookish air refreshes you
as you stand training
your gaze; think about
recycling abuse
hurled at the bins.
Sky's pink. Raise her arm.
No words. It might take
months of weathering
to forget a whisper. Dozens of

mini-deaths to kick-start a voice.
Twisting of wrists and spirit
to free the feet, pump up
a syllable. And screaming
inwardly, down through seasons,
to cut loose one wet-eared
vowel—*see the Muse lean
forward, quivering*—
lengthen and round an 'O'.

Squirming down seasons,
to shuck one rough-cased
vowel—*see her lean
in, quivering*—
one long and trembly 'o'.

asthma-breaths to re-train a
voice, vinegary retching at sins,
oh-see-dee tics, dumb glutting of
thoughts, to plump up the
syllables teeming down seasons
which finally free a howl—spawn
and expel one soulish *'oh!'*.

Which she bends back
to steal with a kiss.

Amanita phalloides

how suddenly & completely
the body   must be   displaced
for sound to carry, sound's medium

orchard-splay in marrow-light

tropic blazon   circumambient
pericarp: compressed as

effigy : mirror : effigy : mirror &

irreducible   the milkynight vowels
converge, speech makes possible

a magnetizing faith   a Providence
creosoted   rime of salt
breathes through/past the lips in their

precise halations, tidal
Florentine, —is not   Artifact

though we possess   & call
the image flickers, each   declivity
of light   distressed   plasmic

unbitten signature the skin collects

in chorus: acclaim as border   crossing:

    we know science

introjects, abstract, sweet   (sphere)

of death at the edge of the meadow

Cwm Gwaun

through alder carr   the west-water sweet-
honey-tongued   flood, Jacob's Well

a Palestine   wooded past & through
the new year, bolt   returned to its horse
or house of   minor forgery,
mossed & fungible   *O severed Emperor*

dissilient, great in age   the flocks tumble
into entymology,   *painted lady, peacock*

flame anent   this rick-haven's
sovereign movement   construed &
what flowered   there, ancient (of days)

vs. clastic asylum   minstered, shadblown

seethe of wild garlic   what haste
can't manufacture, the hand's   merit a low

brother, fractal   haulm encircling
the valley's gorget   milk-blazon regnant

eloigned & carious—   its glass whip—
not for hire this   pricketed (R)evolution

Green Tenor Fire Song

   lit taper of the black bear's body
mauve sheath of tongue
   around the blueberry's charry branch

burn cygnet o burn shingle oak o

   web of carbon, lynx
in the middle distance reconnoiters
   the heart's yurt's thin echo   *(–o)*

burn goshawk o burn signature fawn

   strum of the body's vertical bud
hymning swarm at the creosote pole
   microtuning ozone fan

o fiddlehead o darkling seep
measures midnight's bright bitumen

(I saw the marten for a moment
        before it saw me
(& felt indecent)) —the body's scarf

burn terrapin burn suttler's moss
   o circumflex o veery thrush *(alive-o)*

Feast of St Manaccan
Samuel Shirk, 1936-2011

you who believed in
love's love

depart now   drink
sweet   the dreaming

hand   or planished
motion   on your

body   rests an-
other, smaller mask
for the body's body

placed aside
and then replaced

your love's   love
your body's   body

('s stone setting)

as a torn garment
is lightly cast   aside

on a spring day

on a gray throne

and then recollected
heavy under

dusk's spooring dew

White Work

'A form of embroidery worked with white thread on white fabric.'
      —Royal School of Needlework

I am invested in plain seams, functional edges bound to prevent
fraying, truthfully sewn. The facts. These loose threads hemmed
around the commonplace for a purpose. It is pointless you arguing for
the stability of satin cross-stitch, their disingenuous little histories.
Nobody pays for gold and silver to be conservative. I sicken at the
floss of it, the twist and count, knotted in cerise, gimped in rose.
And the slyness of your white stitch on white linen, the innocent
excision of threads from the ordinary: here it is, you protest, my
honest handiwork simple as your everyday stitches, perhaps just an
accent or two in ecru or ivory.

Normal is a knuckle

says my father

> *So I become a new species*
> *unhuggable as owls*

Normal is a knuckle
said *his* father
he fought with his
bare fists

> *I have plucked my name*
> *from the Book of Apples*
> *at the river of Family I fly*
> *a dove with an army*

Normal is a knuckle
says my father
you knuckle down
or you knuckle
under

> *I become a hateful punch and judy*

> *gird myself with oranges*
> *and information*
> *revel in enormous cities*

> *I moan with love for the horrible*

> *I gnaw on the bone*

Ray DiPalma

The Failure of Specifics

crucibles alembics pelicans stills and bellows

1
Silver and mercury are first
dissolved separately in carefully
measured amounts of *aqua fortis*

the consequent solutions are then
concentrated over hot ashes
obtained from foreign coals

after reducing their volumes
to half the two liquids are
combined in a clay crucible and
exposed to the rays of the sun

2
2000 hens eggs are hardened
in huge pots of boiling water
the shells are carefully removed
and gathered into a great heap
these are then heated in a soft flame
until they are white as snow

the remaining whites and yolks
are separated and putrefied together
in the manure of white horses
the products are distilled and
redistilled for the extraction of
a mysterious white liquid and a red oil

Pictures at an Excavation

                                The sun is wrong—
as if it was only now—as if *when* was finished
though still facing both ways—*when* alone in the shade
of these scattered unwanted remains—
must have got a cramp no one heard the shouts they could say—
never what they think never what they know only what they suspect

Disgust is consequence in the service of repetition
getting it all down while casting aside the pell mell and aging
for emphasis for analysis all very corrective
all very lifelike it deeply engages attribution without remorse
coded **UPON DELIVERY** declared late and poorly
"Thus" being spoken *after* the fork in the road is taken—
bleak with detail and dread familiar themes
the air thinner here at the front of the line—so many

The Select

Too well known to require comment
With reasonable assurance but not certainty
Enunciation determined by imperfect attention
—What remains, he asked
The second and third parts of something
That never existed, he was told
A crowded motif intervening
Neither an accumulation of detail
Nor a mound of stones for throwing
But a protraction of knots—
Of thin air there is no story until now
A visual legacy meant to be disclosed
Only to the uninvited friend
Who had no idea the door would be locked

The detective's name was Swami
He had never wanted the job ['employment stupefies']
His anonymity held a little distance from distraction
A carefully measured distance
Awaiting its rumored inhabitants
Their subtle fingers and more subtle heels
Horrible threats are whispered
Suspense is in the craving
And the intelligence of the notorious
Classic pharmacopoeia and lust
Infractions of the long concealing
Such critical signals are not elusive
But once disclosed they will never reappear
All the imagined difference only an introduction

Like an Umlaut Over a Good Window

Looking out onto a bright street
Those minor mysteries of an ailing ego
Peril and crisis in the service of a miracle

Though hearing, stops and goes all about
This was the adversary, this was the mystery
A reflection and no man, one woman, enough
To know the difference alone somewhere, else

Name the darkness, sir
One meant to be looked at
From above the darkness

Cento [Another Part of the Decimal, for RC]

Though half is   emphasis explicit
in the shifting   what had been
celebrating return   is a door
in the middle   a line to this interval
echoes in   unequivocal involvement
in itself then and the same   over and over
what else   will return says to tell
particulars   give back who knows which
places and minds   seen in the mirror
there's enough   that wants an altered form
of the old rhythms   the congruence of one's own
accounted for   less than the expected sympathy
the natural courtesies   inclined to melancholy
printed on heavy card   baroque principles
and random cruelty   the balance of our response
no more than one plus one   accomplishes the rest
reflex perversity   complex as speed to one standing still
misdirection   for the sake of a preferable cadence
no slang rotting in the corners   of a nervous anecdote
an almost magical discretion   with the contours of paraphrase
something that could not go on   its powers of concealment
no more than one plus one   affords two plus two

from 11781 W. Sunset Blvd.

Credit Card Reader

The only reading worth knowing
step towards the people carrier
ready to meet & capture this World
a grainy figure picks out street angels
pimp or punter hard to tell behind the windshield,
when the cars growl past my window
as the lone power-tool suddenly shuts off,
the naturally benign climate to LA
full of freeways & car interiors
with fixtures hard enough to bang my head into,
granulated neighbourhoods
watch the housing projects from surveillance footage
palm & fig trees, the gated communities.
This is Rilke calling collect from Los Angeles.

10/22/11

My last shave, when? Wednesday?
No, Thursday, before take-off. Two days' growth.
My friend Guy bringing Robert Crosson across from the dead,
heroic, a fine task, sleek in those black
Seismicity Editions—*Day Books* . . . .
with Gaddafi's execution, NATO enters its 'over watch period,'
& we can be glad of the minimal collateral damage
& no NATO or American casualties, the causality
of which means, erce, 'the most successful operation
of Modern Times,' the casual rhetoric of the robotic U.S. military,
relaxed for National Public Radio, informs you & me,
no doubt without tie & top button undone, in his 501s
closer 'To The People,' voice of one, who is one of us.

Hummingbird

Sat at the window tuned to Sunday traffic
where are the drivers rushing
to their limitless gods over limitless tarmac
LA defines the horizontal—no bar, no limit
no known impediment, the grid
Rilke searching streets & corners, passing
cars like the grind of sharpening knives

Chandler's 'The Little Sister'

Relax beside the pool, palms, Scots pine not
now but next
                the magnolias, tankers,
muscle cars, the thirst & appetite
inexhaustible for 24-hour neon artificial
sun, LA as far West as it goes before
becoming East
                        again, heading towards
Santa Monica up Route 405
'the beach is three miles that way,'
the cab driver jabbed his thumb left
& West.

Windshield

iPhone pointing west on Sunset
smog swirls up from the coast
the zombie convoy of Corvettes,
Camaros, Trans-Ams—a wave
sweeps over West Sunset Blvd.
to the STOP sign, & my feet,
this long haul long hop deep

breath, crossing the concrete
the red hand held up, eight
seconds

Commute

home space   —>   work space
in-car time-space the distance
to the office with my name on it
'SIMON SMITH H-462-44'
something something vacant
lot something something
Garnett's photos of Lakewood living
space, 'pragmatic solutions
to the problems of shelter,'
like printed circuitry
a white Mustang ('66?) rolls up
Sunset from Santa Monica
& the beach, the traffic
rolls with it, sucked up on rollers

Brentwood

Writing the 'business' of Hollywood
the blue pool & blue, blue sky
politics laid down beside
the World stopped, all a-shimmer
drive up Wilshire you cross Euclid
grid not geometry to human
scale of break down into the drag
racer's day, trade in
my 501s for a *Pacific Standard Time*
catalog, five pea eem.
Sun strong then night. Dark, cold.

There is no climate in LA
there is no weather in San Diego,
flip the thermostat, chill, adjust.

Long Distance

Drive, & you take part, face life
face lift & the pure products
of the dream factory
we met at the intersection, drive
in, feel free, the printed circuit,
the 'lift' accept no
substitute, the elevator
a surgical procedure to capture
youth in face of the Other

An Email for David Herd: Anna's Hummingbird

Its flickering bright
                        body green then yellow then
one
        corporate environment
to the next
             red Camaro
flips lanes
            the hypodermic
bill, the Getty marble
-facings of High Modernism
air con on   I reach out   see
through   beyond   my thinking mid-sentence
                this grid of a notebook
the streets & drawn blinds   the boundaries
drawn down   capillary action   high above
the clouds like spaceships   boomerangs or flat-irons
the perimeter road   its razor-wire, dogs

you need a code—   zip, genetic, pin
a surgical strike on red
blossom   the Armed Response
of the Bel-Air Patrol   sucking up nectar
thru the epistemology of lime and lemon
Maseratis sip stamen to stamen   the cul-du-sac
                         of show cars
on the beach @ Malibu
where your working day ends
mine begins, you can reach me
a new email address & Anna's Hummingbird
browsing for fructose   & walking is thinking not driving
a brace of pelicans flap across

W. Pico

Cameras tree to tree
police the walkers & care
for our freedom the silver Elantra sedan
affords us, registration 5HFE080
on a California plate, hire
car dropping transmission oil
to the drive
tick tock tick tock tick tock
indicate, then veer to the left lane exit
up the up ramp, then down the down
flat slabs concrete sky
snug to concrete road the grey abandoned
buildings something something something
fits something to something & something

Out of Malibu

& Jim Rockford's Pontiac
cold case re-opened
Black Dahlia to the Zodiac Killer to Natalie Wood
a rainbow over LA
Downtown the pot
of gold & 14400 Sunset
Dennis Wilson's, see Manson slips
away the picture right, shadow
door to wall, and the singer stopped
breathing, surf boards propped
& golf courses manicured, we're neat
in line for chips &
soda, the return
to normal life & a be em double ya
chill to Chet Baker's
'The Thrill
is Gone'
looming with the rain
clouds over LA way too far
a city too big to fail
its up to the jury, you file your report back
to English money
the 747 tips around one eighty
out of the Pacific
the hundred Croydons of the west
& time before
the slip down across to Greenwich
the Meridian & one last 'hello' to LA
01:47 tomorrow from 17:47 today

ALICE MILLER

After Battle

This stitching between bodies isn't skin.
It's only old rope, easily cut.

Where the seam tears there's blood.

I found a body under the trees,
thrown from its horse.

I wrapped taut silk around its bones
and watched the rivers roam the roads.

It was just me and the body.

I pretended it lived, and together we listened
to the sly sounds between trees.

*

I want you to come here,
restitch your head to your shoulders,
and form a word with your soft mouth.

Come here and surrender.

Because there're still days that my army
loses horses, days I lose sun
    and try to saddle up the darkness—

*

and whenever we ride to battle together, it rains
and we cannot see sky for water,
and the grass becomes dirt, and

waves break the fields, and the bodies
all muddle into the earth.
And although your breath

was once pressed into mine,
I no longer know who's against me.

Album of Breath

While the record plays? Should I say: Brahms-
loved-Clara, wrote each note for her, his
best friend's wife, after Robert'd thrown himself

into the Rhine, and recovered then raved
till death did-he-part? Do these snaps—one composer
gone mad, in a river; one beauty doing

as beauty always does; and one Brahms, a pianist
whose hands stretched
two octaves (I do not know how far

a madman's hands might stretch)—and to refer
to Schumann as the madman—
Does this make these notes, we hear now, better,

or make us the epicentre
of a massive city
where nothing has ever happened?

JAMES McLAUGHLIN

Imaginings

—will I take these words to a heightened register
assume a condescension as green as the earth green

    roll over lakes and fields

we were too young to know the truth
that the spring would only last a while

picking flowers and throwing them in the fire

you sat leg in leg looking straight at me
two eyes dark—black as a heart

    in each new day there are beginnings
some hope for an amber sky—perhaps

at night I still dream of life
      over and over
    a neurosis that feeds on imagining—
flamed to a molten ponytail—stark regret

    that solitary day by the river
the sun
  on the golden hill
      and you white   soft
as flesh

flesh

Choruses

—your choruses were all so silent (always)—continuous
like yard stones standing by graves
rows of them— a city
away off somewhere I hear a magpie or
is it a distraught fiend

it was a frigid look you gave me
and a white note fell into my hand

selection is the range from which the stars fall
a fantastic arrangement of finalities
the genetics and processes by which we adapt
environments producing offspring resulting in the gradual

Love is such a gambler I saw that in your eyes
felt it on your gifted brow and cool hand

was it nine inches of blade you gave me
or did the moon die on the tide—was
I mouthing like a babbling child calling *muma*
then you fell limp as the light

Master

—at various times we may arrive at conclusions
diffident in dreams new born without disguises
we cannot tolerate what internal voices may tell us
listen to the instincts that might make us rejoice

I shun the rain that has swept all day in the woods
taken shelter in streams and dendritic undergrowth

wrap a warm blanket of neglect round my shoulders

and if they will not tell me I will ask—take to one side
that black sky up there with a hint of a pale blue eye
whisper in its ear—then run down the gaunt valley
cadaverous and ungiving under foot

you have always taken the principal role pushed
your dire punishments to the point of tragedy—compelled bent
double before your pupil—it is a pivotal role—
that pain

the small sharp metal pin that sewed my skin
holing a thread in my cheek

will you ever leave me to this quiet day to
the succulent sound of the water—to the frozen air
on the cherry that contorts its broken branches

At Fifty

I.
At fifty if I look I've been fifty
        years excavating my own language
                from inside to deeper inside

look at me don't look at me no odds
        common grave of wakeful dream
                a band of laughing clean-shaven souls

childhood a braid of bright ribbon
        fraying around a sheaf of sacred images
                & the ergot of saints' haloes

pale veins racing out the body
        to lick frosted moonlight off paving stones
                in the green shade of white procession torches

fear of language red smoke cut with desert sand
        diamonds in my throat I had to cut
                spectrum of song for the beam of breath

light in august the bulb burning the eyes
        the nightmare visitations at break of day
                buzzing terror of black letters on gold pages

ladies of the lake mascara queens
        old mistresses at fifteen lipsticking wisdom
                on mirrors & curtains of sunlit smoke

poetry the bunch of keys worn round the neck
        the singed skirt the bright odd stockings of stripes & lace
                the roses & thorns loosed out the hair

              o requiem aeternam lover girl

wheat sheaf of wasted wedding songs
  jewels offered up to the lords of dawn
    bonfire snows & shivered invocations

o river of all giving
    polish this stone I am

o scythe of moon reborn
    bleed me of the truth until I shine

        *

royal rookeries of shit & bleach
  of soap & boiled rice & fossil flowers
    we rule the world with our crowns of white heat

royal gardens of thorn & acorn
  of ivy & dead rosewood & sick-scarred elder
    we rule the world with our crowns of berry black

sulphur & mother's milk, seed & obsidian
    the body's craving for ritual

the paradox of aging the body turning
    more delicate as it coarsens

poetry the long summer fasts the pollen of the chest
    the eyes washed white by tears
     —you better have some fun jimmybones

come with us don't come with us no odds
  we have bodies like fishbones or mossy caves
    we have minds with long wild manes & we eat

    weather.

We spell out the work ethics of derangement
        spin a dervish web on the edge of bankrupt nerves
                or flog the poisons of the flesh for cash while dreaming

of one rainbow body rising from two adjacent
           installations of nerve bone & blagged streetwear
                      —you think I'm joking I know

but our last words of love are
        do what you want or we'll break you

           exploration is for those with a measure of peasant blood

*

rotten orchards of city money logic
        festering vineyards of broken ancestral pride
                labouring engine of earth hatred & heartbreak

shrines of broken glass
        by the highway of roadkilled language

rhumb line of the body on the sea of death
        rhumb line of language on the ocean of images

young men singing like belling deer
        & below deck poisoned angels cutting deals
                hard against lost memories of fresh water

don't sit down you twisted old demon no bargain
        say she opens her body to the filth of your mourning
                what gold will you bring to the harvest of sight

the honey of night's not enough
        for this here my daughter of birdsong & dew
           —away with you

forsaken diorama of high theatre wrath
  black lantern excavating darkness seeking

incalculable irreducible delicacy
  a spider thread of music
    waterfalling its sure way into the heart

exhaustion & completeness of the nerves
  an invisible wall of music
    we lean against like two unfinished paintings

To the Source

sourse

sourdre to rise

surgere–

walk with me
follow the green
through the dry oaten grass
the green of nettles, thistles, clover, sorrel,

the dampness
where condensation rolls
over the dip and the swell
of the land
rinsing through Bagshot sand and layers of flint,
funnelled into the welt
of Chalybeate

leaching horizontally over thin clay beds
to spring from the navel
as that *wyllspring*.

run-off tethered into rills and rivulets
rivus
reiwol
rei–

flowing
through the puddled ponds
of *Caen-wood*,

sinking that deep surge
cold as hell,
in the lake of guilt
pulling
under Parliament Hill

the eastern stream
straumaz, stram
strom, stroom, sreu–

willing its confluence
with the western branch
hulled from the Vale of Health,

the tranquil pond
so still
and painful,

a perfect circle of water-lilies
imperceptible
its drift   idling

through the dense underlay,
horsetail, reed, bulrush and sphagnum moss,

the ooze picking up momentum
into the hollow stream

Oldbourne, Holburna, Holbourne
whittling south-east

becoming the river Fleet
fleotan, fleot, fl_ot,
flod

at Anglers Lane.
Caen-ditch Town
Ken-ditch town

anchor of the Thames
at its tidal reach

This Silent Mist

This silent mist could never quite
obliterate the distance since
a frailer silhouette of trees (grey-
wrapped to shroud that yellowing)
stays in the eye as something caught
imperfectly by memory
if hardly recognised as such—
a clumsy Rorschach Test, asymmetrical,
half leaf-torn, like an amateur attempt
to trace a Chinese ideograph on
to damp cloth.
                Those kanji learnt so doggedly
at Naganuma's forty years
ago
     (pausing somewhere in Shibuya
for beer and sushi after an a.m. making
the economic students—all male—laugh
at limericks then with the Eng.
Lit. class—all female—sauntering through
some Yeats)
              are dwindling slowly week
by month by year by lack of practice plus
dark disobedience of the brain.

One I still pen from time to time to please
the gullible or mystify the bored means
dragons on the move—a handy sign
to warn the smug or timid about change
or danger lurking—and it takes
forty-eight strokes to make it though
you only really need to cram the first
design which equals *dragon* (sixteen
strokes) three times into a tiny square:

a wise precaution for (who knows?)
they might fly off again to chase
the flaming pearl or churn the clouds
to curdled ebony. The third St. John
(aka The Divine) foresaw captive dragons
lifting off to wreak their havoc briskly since
they know they have "but a short time".
(It's also claimed they never tell the truth.)

Old address-books still clasp homes and names
of those no longer reachable
down here or where we are. It's cruel
to cross them out for they possess
identities beyond the haze
left by each swift decade. Who now
can make the black receiver ring
Cheam in the 1930s with
VIGilant one-o-double-eight? In fact
you'd get the vanished garage (Surrey Motors) by
mistake. A word plus number stays
far easier to recall than just
a tedious string of digits but
that's by the way and I'm too old
(I'm told) to grasp how all
is altering for the better while
unarmed protesters out to make
tyrannical régimes resign
get shot, too few Samaritans
will lug the wounded to a hostel
using their credit-card to pay
maybe for harbouring a corpse
and greedy firms contrive to turn
tap-water flammable by fracking.

On sleepless nights my left palm forms
a desk to scrape syllabaries
the way, back in Japan, they scrawl
the pattern of a tricky surname

for some uncomprehending friend.
There'll be a couple I've forgotten—*ne*
perhaps in hiragana, florid, flowing, though
confused at times with *wa* or *re*—or else
the katakana sign for *ru*
but never *ge su to* for they're
my name. (Nor *ha ri i* either. What
a privileged concision!) Lynn's
rin kanji shows a delicate pair of trees,
a splash of water to the left. One could
translate those printed drips
to mist and drape the double trees
in half-translucent mystery for once.

"What gets my goat," proclaimed the Dragon
Chief who answers (sometimes) to the name
of Xrohvaah, "is gettin' called a bloody serpent.
"Fella up on Patmos started the wretched rumour.
"Rotten show." Jet claws glint as
they're flexed. A whiff of mustard-
coloured smoke issues from one nostril. "Dammit.
"We're in a taxonomic class all by ourselves.
"Never have been. Always will be."

Dream up a skyscraper to hold
whatever should be fixed inside
the skull—a lofty warehouse, sort
of archive-guarder with a cache
of faded letters, playscripts, sepia
photos, scribbled drafts, lists which have lost
all meaning, notebooks indecipherable.
A willing lad's in charge, snub-nosed
with cheerful freckles, keen to help
the self bemused who's found the term
or memory he wants either beyond the tongue
or crouched behind a maddening fact
too similar to risk dismissing out
of hand. Why should a word you know

the sense of fail to phrase itself?
The title of a novel I've just read
escapes me. Who was the thug
who played the sidekick in a favourite Western?
That blonde girl now. What was her name?
I waltzed with her on some
illuminated dance-floor underneath
the stars—a chequer-board flicking her skirt
from dark to scarlet. Salzburg. 1950.
(Ah! Hilde Gueden's Cherubino!)
The answers (if they come) require a time-
lag till embarrassingly e.
g. *abstemious* leaves the lips
by vicious chance occurring next
morning in the crossword slotting in
with *crab, Tasmania, hoo-ha* and *dissent.*
That breezy landowner on Guernsey—
he must have had a name—called crosswords
"mental masturbation" but if Perec
liked to set them as a hobby that's
all right by me.
                    And those vague oaks
aren't figments. Mist arching (walls
and roof of monochrome) makes all
unreal labelled or not. A buzzard, damp
and hunched, sits the still weather out.
I wonder where I am not who
unlike the day on Dartmoor when I walked
from one stone row to sudden
fog heading for a forest gone invisible
with confidence which lessened when
I neared no trees
                    and then I saw
one monolith looming in a world
of nothing and I knew I'd made
unwittingly an awkward circle on
rough grass unseen just sensed beneath
my soles.

Dragon wings beating might
have blown the wet opacity away
but on that wintry day alone
none seemed around.
                        Dredging
from nowhere the blank fact. To send
my freckled friend off scurrying
up stairs, down corridors, past stacks
of magazines, piled crates to seek
the relevant filing-cabinet.
                            It takes
sometimes an hour, sometimes a day and soon
it may be never. What I longed to see or say
to memorise or wonder at—
even misunderstand—will lie
in dust. My non-existent snub-
nosed server will not even rank
as ghost. What trivial splendour may
linger among those heaps
of alien matter to be chucked
in the incinerator or get crushed
for landfill? No mystery can be
a mystery until it's known
as such so time will scribble out
those painted oaks, conceal the perching bird,
censor the poem, crack the sculpture,
mislay the glowing ruby, silence
the nascent song and let
the fog and captious dragons have their way.

Linda Black

She Walks for Days

Up and down stairs   in and out
the washing machine   has become
where she is where the moon got her
She has nowhere   goes by foot
tripping over her own worse for wear
explains nothing   doesn't admit   she is not
of that faith   It is many years ago now
she turned and walked away   no thought
from her own good someone else's
consequence & the madman   inside
where ten pinafores hang

What a clever thing she just did
she calls people she hasn't seen for years
she is proud!   when she leaves
the first time is seriously threatened
bump bump bump   headfirst
on the back wheels   As no one has told
and no one is so all day this thing
from out of her propped upright

A saviour in a soft jumper
or her sister's skin   she has no clear
picture   apart from preferring
long fingers   In that seated posture
did Keats have long fingers?   a balanced
book   a crossed knee   *but ...*
she corrects herself   One hand is
one head was   then retracts
too much of a put down
a regency chair   but it could be

The air comes up against her
has extremities   both she covets
she covets both   under the carpet
looking out   all she can see
is space   she does not want a box
gathering   what she incorporates
would anyone?   She stays inside
hers   sometimes venting

All day it puzzles her
from dwelling   How exactly?
a slight   small and precise
remembered from life   to another
what she couldn't herself   the same words
repeated in the future   very slight
changes   not circles exactly

A good few years ago he told her
like a beam she imagined   a searchlight
from out of the top of her head   then
about the needles   a pincushion
he said   it must have been
unbearable   So many objects
shedding light

Turn to where there is no light
check she is here   she must not
run pell-mell along the side
of the hearth   where the edge
meets the craved way   today
she looks to the sky thinking
to be someone else
A visitor say

Where dazed people live   shy
to the bare branches   shall go somewhere
back to the bare ground   could it be
this is the very same jug
or distant relative?   a chair
transposed   no regard for age
or time   passes quicker
Shall not notice
what her eyes see

Something flimsy
of little input   not cracked up
to be   really very fragile
wrapped in cellophane   distanced
from the swing   the wood
the unnecessary detail

EDWARD MACKAY

We can meet love always
*An erasure poem from the prison letters of Rosa Luxemburg
to Sophie Liebknecht, July 1916–October 1918*

The heat sat down and smiled saying:
I am like so much love.

I cannot change no matter where you go
You send love to endure
to trouble   to unease sorrow.

These sad days seem nothing but love.
Your keen moment ran away   decided to go south.

Picture nothing; neither voice nor the ripple or murmur of wind
in always   in beautiful   in real

go and greet the hunger   to hold pressed against
you
read me the world that remains,   make me burst,

do not understand me,   make me feel free;

stand at midnight,   steeply blue and silent

life is always unsatisfied, looking delight in the eye.

I heard danger, its writhing like music.

I walk in the empty dark

Only love can express a meaning in silence.

I know that the autumn shall seek a return
      rooted in things beyond my shadow

I am full of the life where the days before nothing still live.
I grew remarkable   shook upon lightning

now everything indescribable spread across the sky like a silent call

all these years carry on in impossible liberty.
Now that the door   will be open

Afterword
for Tsutomu Yamaguchi

Twice licked by lightning, this man like a comet
passes twice across the blank pulse of sky to make

his shadow stand, unhitched from flesh, etched to tarmac
and brickwork in two cities, at once. He cannot make time

stop again, as it did twice, the clocks totemic
with their cracks and twice-right times, unravelling meiotic

new light from the old, a world, twice tipped to dark. Commit
again the crime of chance, slough off, again, all yet to come

or live as stains of carbon, chemical scum, the automatic
offspring of unchoosing chance. So choose. Come to

the edge, again, and leap, again: eyes ablaze, atomic.

Trompe l'oeil

The night of research
is over. The ideas have come,
we are judged by an old suit.
The small light on his microphone burns red.

I want to float out,
escape up through that Baroque vault
past stone ramparts into blue
welcome of angels. A woman presses

her idea against
the mahogany barrier
kneading at the sculpted wood.
When she lies down idea-less later,

I would lie in her
arms for ever if that would help her sleep.

Sere and Yellow

I wake to news
of the invasion.

I take the world
in at the ear.

My hands spread
the soil of clothes.

My knees kneel
up to the window.

Soldiers eat
outside our carriage.

White feather
woven of air

that tapped my father's
shoulder, why

don't I fight?
Douaniers

march the crying
men along

the wagon-lit
with plastic bags.

Crested country
encrusted soft

gems of misted
wood. My Croque

Monsieur is cold.
I share with metal

the waste of rust,
this force that smacks

a bridge apart,
fizzes paint

in bits of plunder,
sheds its own

September, piece
by piece by piece.

Homage to Avraham Ben Yitzhak

Between the Name of the Patriarch
and of his Son, the Poet

is silent, an intervening Angel.

Somebody tells me
the only Person who spoke the Lord's

Name was the Mother
of the Poet's Double.

Did the Poet and the Father
build the Kaa'bah?

Or did their Doubles?
I thought God had Ninety-Nine Names?
The Unpronounceable: *To not create the First Person.*

Yet to build a Second House…

Later, a Descendent of the Double
would return to the Festival of Poetry

to empty the House of Images,
make an Image of Emptiness.

Where in the argument are the 'Satanic Verses'?

Then, centuries later, in Vienna's Café-Museum,
the Names of the Son and the Patriarch

wouldn't be enough to return
the Poet to Being;

his Father passed away,
his Mother's home razed,

his lost writings had been replaced
by twelve anonymous poems.

Let his Name be Unwritten, as he wished.

Let his Silence be an echo
of these, his words:

"On seven roads we depart and on one we return."

The Aryan Face of Nefertiti
after Martin Bernal

Black, like the doorway
between the Mosque of the Soul
and the Pilgrims' Hostel
of the Face: Athena's

assumed visage, as the Ace
of Spades, no less there
than Nefertiti in her avatar,
Hitler's beloved statue.

They say, when the Ancients
painted a face black
they meant 'fertile'… An Afrikaner
poet once wrote: *Poets are born black,*
whitening with age.

The Copts

There, where two fingers
would find a pulse,

on the inside of his wrist,
he has the Coptic Cross

tattooed, a vital sign,
an amulet, almost secret,

like a word, Pharaonic,
surfacing to remain in Arabic,

a voice, calming, calling
across centuries of noise.

Cats of Zamalek

Universal are the cats
of Zamalek, 'at once',
as the English say, the kitten
toying with Mumbai rubbish, licking
the sauce off a take-away wrapper
and a mummified beast,
yellow eyes glinting emerald
at that nanosecond when we stumble
on Time. Universal these cats,
if miniature. Our presence
in passing is exaggerated,
colossal, sphinx-like
only in ruin.

Chapter one

After a moment's opportunity
A strangled collection   of stones
From the words: "I'd like to stay"
In the gentle swell of plain

whistling through Teeth
as an eager child
bright with open bunches
stealing a cloud

peeling words off eyes
drunk from cupped hands
from a world of living
folded across the chest

stiller than thought
noticing the sunlight
in a swollen 'hush'
they turn without speaking

and your hard pushed to imagine
a smaller voice in the purse of appetite
passing lips—they'll go on denouncing
like hours that want to stop:

twisting, holding, stammering
close but not touching
struggling through layers of detail
within the rim of what's shared

chapter four

by assuming a postulate
I presume the possible
The purpose of making
On a scale of great magnificence

To me extraordinary
With the power of choosing
By likenesses clear & remote
Let it not be forgotten

In a halo of phases
Suggested by my own experience
Opening a hemp o' gossamer
as parts or symbols of truth

 that the intuition of geometry
that *spake as a dragon*
in fragments wild
& the transits of wanderers

without loss of time
compelled the consequence
of feeling in my eyes
where histories detail

ground to a paste & stones
shaped the density of *something-
nothing-everything* a playmate
of the waves supported by a song,

that lives compressed
 & folded by a process
 squeezed in the in
escapable vice of love.

chapter five

i.m. Maddy Hobson

You are looking into my eyes
As though I am there

You are thinking of me
Somewhere floating still
on the wild open
Withholding the truth

That the heart leads nowhere
That the eye has reached its own horizon
But a thought steals into the darkness
And you surround me everywhere

And every dew/ continually
Sought in tender shoots
Shows you there/ conceding
Your every cell to the night

Chapter thirteen

Perhaps there should be more love in your poetry,
Miniaturising oceans so they are smaller than grain.

Perhaps when the moon is full, you could settle there
Conjuring a universe the size of another piece of grain.

It seems to me that all these things are small, love, I mean,
Is tiny like a dream, & much less than the substance of grain.

If I was to give you advice, you would have to cherish it &
hold it in an hour glass—each breath a history for each grain.

I remember when I was a grain, the moments seemed less
And the willing was inaudible, and did you know that each grain
Was surrounded by a pocket of air, very individual, yet together
We had the strength of a surface; we moved each and every grain
With the tide along the river, but many times we came to settle.

So many grains became a continent/ so many loves against the grain.

Speaking About the Henge

We stopped and parked then
strict as wings
the jackdaws threw their sound against the stones
it ricocheted as lines of glass
as shining shining shining shining tricks of triple k
the stones sent back the sound as stings of song
that broke the sun to spokes
that spoke the day or was it
A calendar of sun and throat ofsunandthroat
hung here.

     At the interactive museum and shop
     we learned that before the henge
       a tangle of dense oak had spread across the downs.

     How broad those branches must have been
     with leaves as constellations of light and sap
     in miles of lacing arcs that tracked the sun.

we learned that forests are green weight
               held heeled holed
by the gravity of song
that they are   folds
of budding stars, spiraling and lobed
           fixed

by the voice of blackbirds

in the clarity of groves

we were walking back towards the car when

lax as wings

a blackbird spilt its song over the grass

> It worked the paradox of light and voice
> that deals with flight and weight's dense curse
> and when it was as sure as stones it looped a course
> above our heads and gently took the sun apart
>
> Our guide book said that blackbirds ranged in woods
> and these were gone that trees were howked by spades of bone
> to clear a space for time's new hoax and what
> was left were tricks of stone the uprights aping oaks

we learned that at this place of slash and burn

event was made

an uptight marking of place and turn

that song, chakked from the necks of daws, prisms

that this was a site of lithic modernism

Tangled with chirrup and fruit

On a breakneck of rocks
Tangled with chirrup and fruit,
Froth, flute, fin, and quill

Dylan Thomas

And in those years
it was always late November—bare
dove grey, then darker: woollen must and briefly surfacing light,
and in those years I pinned the days
with shapes of trees and mostly this one:
Wind smeared, toppling
with the toppling wall; a stagger and a yearn for the long horizon;
spined and hard with berries little more than stones made crimson
          with a shine,
but mostly made soft with birds that changed the whole blurred
          thorny smear
to panicked song as I walked past to school.

I didn't have the words until I was fully grown.
Those stones, those birds, those panicked spines,
I found them in a book which quietly had kept for me
the briefly surfacing shine: that long and lit horizon
of the calm and waiting line.

Galata Bomb 2003

You said you saw the street made Christmas with the shine
of broken things that split the light—
of objects cut and loosed before their time.

Lamp making Beyoglu streets unwind
through coloured glass and hammered wire,
you said you saw these streets made Christmas with the shine;

that small ponds and balanced bones inside
your head had thickened with the thickened air, now twice
as dense with objects cut and loosed before their time.

The street had grown from site to sight
a lengthening of the world so bright
you said you saw the street made Christmas with the shine

and you had grown from I to eye
a lengthening of the vowel so slight, pulled by
the weight of objects cut and loosed before their time.

And now, despite
the lack of lamps, night after glassy night
you say you see that street made Christmas with the shine
of objects cut and loosed before their time.

PETER ROBINSON

The Passers-By

'naturally the public mind was demoralized'
—Walter Bagehot, *Lombard Street*

1. Grey Squirrel

A squirrel in Russell Square garden
advances across russet leaf-fall,
not at all shy
of us, passing by.

Pertinent glances identify
his way back through the hedge;
white flashes edge
a mousy tail.

While that glimpse of hotel frontage
brings out your hoarded lifetime,
there's overcast sky
in his beady eye.

Ear twitched at the light-change roar,
he catches up some of his store
and with arched spine
makes a beeline

through wind-turned leafage, yet more
traffic noise, lit dust, when as per
usual crowds swarm
past us, going home,

and we're gone from the square.

2. A Tramp-Barge

Plumes of smoke from the chimneystack
on a tramp-barge stream above
the path between two waterways
at Jericho; here it's hunkered down
as if for winter or the hard times coming.
Moored, kitted out with a bike or two,
heaped firewood, pot plants, that barge huddles up
in its shawl of black tarpaulin.

Then there's something in you drawn to it
as scents of fry pan bacon come
wafting on the rain-fresh air …
How it takes its chances for survival!
Aloof, anonymous, autonomous—
or it seems so to the likes of us
taking a wrought-iron bridge across
this slow canal in autumn.

3. The Eye

If front-of-house have lost the plot
and are corpsing on the spot,
well, behind the scenes
better actors learn their lines
in spoked shadows from a gondola wheel.
Its years of oversight reveal
how funds like surface water,
bird notes, or the air waves' chatter,
are soaked away in daylight.
They can't help corpsing on the night;
and, inimical, you imitate
our *faux amis'* own secret state
of mind—being caught on someone's phone,
documenting demoralization
at the Thames parapet, so
sold downriver by that bank-side flow.

4. Public Space

Ochre tints splotch whitened ground.
An oak-tree sapling stands alone,
late leaves intact in a field of snow.
Look, an identity tag around
its slender bark,
branches and leaves are to grow
in memory of a girl—
her name engraved on the metal plaque.
Etched in frost, that robust
tree resists sub zero
winter bite and gale-force blast.

5. Nativity

Moonlight, glanced off fresh-settled snow,
illuminates our bedroom
in what must be a waking dream
with its faint, unearthly glow.
Circled by purple crayon,
your stigmata of keyhole surgery
at navel and abdomen,
they take me back to the same old story.
It's our long disgrace in other terms
on gallery or chapel wall—
depicted cruelties, grieving, harms
livid at abdomen and navel
now a bleak mid-winter warms
to its being told again, again for our survival.

n'Bytsje

A seventh spring and still
I miss some arcane step
beside me through the wood,
while seedlings seek their secret
names you knew, and in the
quickening a tiny bride
trills her shy song in your
lost tongue—n'bytsje, n'bytsje—
how is she called who flitting
sweetens with her speech
the still that lies between
us now n'bytsje, how?

Half by Half We Sleep

On this eve of nativity
twined lovers stranded high
above tideline on shore
of age-stroked stones a gift,
a present each to each

beneath far rainbow doubly born
of brine, cord cast uncut
into blue noon like diadem
of neonate studded with news
to shake the snow-streaked hills

and half by half we sleep,
watched over by the same veiled nurse
and half by half we wake
to the becoming of the universe.

On Maximos' *The Dormition of the Theotokos*

In the frame where you lie, I sit upright.
>One minute at the intersection of repose,
>terrible lines on lateral light.
How to sit?
>When we will right very still eyed
bring or send a censor, then a scent,
our final estimation of your weight.

In the colors of two identical icons
the hands of Mary do not match her face.
>Just as the enclosure of two fabric planes
>does not allow us really to feel indoors.
We see a blind wilderness contained
within a mattress and two solid hands
make an arbitrary whiteness.

I admit with embarrassment that I cannot lift you,
>and
>an impulse of disability
presses the farthest away layer of my skin.
The line of your shoulder is a human faculty—
sitting upright.
>And I have a weakness for faculties.

If duplicated enough times, any pair of eyes
will begin to look foreboding.
>Resting over an intersecting line
>of this last flexible light.
For, I am persuaded, even now,
of the flatness of your features,
and the ill-will of the chiaroscuro.

I remember how we were not quite in a circle
and how come you never added any depth.

This lack of foreground refers traditionally
to the dimensions of shame, the lack of musculature
in the voice that pronounces foreign names.
　　　　A cleft palate is not a double jointedness,
it does not become two mouths
or a divided subjectivity.
There is no compensatory model
for the loss of a velar stop.

I repose into the shape you will remember.
　　　　To sit upright,
to suddenly on a sudden,
　　　　　　to really on a real,
be very truthful.
　　I curl into creases, folding, frivoling, face to lace, lingering tombs and
　　　　　wounds wound airily to the ground.
Then I will be unfolding, be beginning to be held.
　　　　There, there. There is many a one.

Untitled

She left glow-in-the-dark stars over my bed
that traffic the ceiling after she's gone,
adhering to the kindness of her intention.
I see in them the history of English spelling
and the morning chasing thorns from her back.

From the Apocryphal Acts of Andrew and Matthias among the Man-Eaters

I.

The pacing of the guard
made the mark of three rows of teeth.
And when he told me to wait
his mouth was like a potted plant.
His dirty potsherd teeth,
they wanted what they wanted.
He spoke in clay to me and told me to wait.

II.

Civil servants with sovereign teeth
   mimic gravel in their speech.
They bundled by wrists my wrists
   and moved me into a knot.

Human eyes derived from scratches
   watch you as you undo statues.
They gathered my mouth in grasses
   and made me into a wall.

III.

Ear-
shaded kings.
East, and heat, east east. I
understand
they carry themselves like streets running with blood.
In Greater Nestoria, magogs broke them in bread. They
were found out.

Rings & Circles

I

The Polymath holds a pencil in his right hand and a blue pen in his left. The eraser sits next to his spec-case and empty Virgin coffee cup. Red, black & green sway in the little office of his jacket pocket and his specs hang low on his nose. In his long fingers the pencil hovers above his diagram like an artist's brush, a conductor's baton measuring time as the train speeds to Aberdeen. The blue pen doubles as a ruler, guiding the dodecahedron through its many metamorphoses. The pencil swoops, inserting dotted rings & semi-circles, arrows, darts & chevrons onto the model—these analogies of space and time across physical and biological structures. He calls it A Model of the Mind and I'm minded of those wondrous childhood atlases that made the earth come alive mapping the great migrations of the natural world—flocks of swans & geese darkening the North American skies, herds of gazelles & wildebeest traversing the great savannahs of Africa, shoals of whales & turtles plying the oceans of the globe.

II

The Art Dealer is travelling too, his spirit fired by a timely opportunity in Hong Kong, where for once he has the money and, he says, even if the world continues its meltdown, will be able to put food on the table and pay the rent. He sends me a jpeg and I fall in love with the thirteen horses. It is said to be an incense-burning altar, unearthed in an excavated tumulus, entering the collections of the tsar in 1716 and now preserved in the Hermitage Museum, St. Petersburg. I carry it in my head on the ferries to the Northern Isles. To Orkney's Neolithic village at Skara Brae, to the circular chambered tomb at Maeshowe, the standing stones at Stenness. I stand in the middle of the Ring of Brodgar, the lochs—once marshland—and surrounding hills glowing in the early sunset. Suddenly the thirty-six still-existing stones transform into thirteen horses cantering round the central hearth. Then, just as abruptly, they turn and gallop away, manes flying, hooves thundering as they begin their return to the great Russian Steppes of 2500 B.C.

Apitherapy

And thy Lord inspired the bee to build its cells in hills, on trees and in men's habitations. There issues from within their bodies a drink of varying colours, wherein is healing for men. AL-QUR'AN 16:68-69

The Scientist buys two jars of the best honey. I sit at my desk, face smeared in liquid gold, waiting for glucose oxydase to combine with my skin-fluid and turn into hydrogen peroxide. Then it will slough
necrotic tissue, speed up granulation and epithelialisation and heal my skin. The doctor pushes my hair from my face but his hand is not a healing hand. He has beautiful eyes—but his steroids don't help and his penicillin has lost its efficacy. He's forgotten that a thousand years ago his ancestors trusted honey's anti-bacterial, anti-inflammatory and analgesic properties. My face is swollen, red and sore. He says that to find the floral source would be a wild goose chase ... but even Hippocrates knew: *honey cleans sores and ulcers of the lips, heals carbuncles and running sores.* It's lip-lickingly good. Delicious on toast, crackers and cake. The Polymath brings me milk and gingerbread. Then he remembers Plutarch. He shuts the window so I'm not a magnet. So I won't suffer the terrible fate of the poor young soldier Mithridates.

Cycles & Wheels

This week the Art Dealer is no longer certain that the Insignia is exclusively Islamic. He needs to find the living Fibonacci of calendar history—one of the few souls alive who can spin and read off Metonic and Callipic cycles as Leonardo read sunflowers. So, as of yesterday he turns like a sunflower to the makers of Swiss watches and just one phone call to Geneva ... I gaze up at the sky as I ride the Poet's shoulders. He starts to spin and I stretch out my arms to the universe, imagine my mind the hub of a wheel, the spokes barely moving as the carriage gathers speed. I try to concentrate, to collect my thoughts into a single point of emptiness, for I've heard that only a vacant space can fill. Now, sitting in the single empty place on a bench in the John Betjeman Arms, St. Pancras, I anticipate the Art Dealer. When he arrives he fills the recently-vacated gap next to me and orders a good bottle of Chilean red. We are so pleased to see each other we hardly notice the ebb and flow. Then he tells me that the space just below his kidney is occupied. Next week he will enter the Clinique St. Paul for the nephrectomy.

Heads & Hats

The Polymath is wearing a straw hat to protect his head. He walks ahead, hands and fingers weaving a rhythm as he composes and conducts. For one who claims he cannot sing he brims with poésies that always sing to me. And even brimless hats can sing. The Art Dealer's bronze Insignia once held a gemstone in its centre and was worn to ornament the red, yellow or purple turban atop a sheikh's noble head. Now the Polymath is saying that the Mexican Hat diagram represents the allowable states in the system and the height is the system's energy and—silly me!—the equilibrium state is the peak of the hat and the minima are just inside the rim of the hat in the form of a complete circle. But all I can see is the photo he took on our honeymoon: twenty-five men in sombreros on the back of a truck somewhere in Chihuahua.

more or less

so as if enough
was, then, enough:
the pause in the tread,
the light fading,
& that scent of woodsmoke
where the path curves up
beyond the trees on the skyline,
or the climb levels off,
so that you think maybe
the view will be rewarding
but the track carries on ever uphill,
seemingly steeper,
as your boots tighten & soles blister
(surely you could have come
better prepared?)

then ahead lies another day of the same
& more days of the same
after night after night
punctuated by mosquitoes

& no theorem to explain this continued tread
the effort involved in getting to the end
of the beginning:

the foot of the wall
where the true climb
hangs
up there
into the clouds

As Nice as It Is, It Isn't

The cliffs in winter. Regret or rejoice?
In the snug, the taps wink,
mirrors reflect long summers
of joy and despair
suns sinking into far horizons
or whatever you dream of.
But here now when it matters
it's all in your hands.

We sit and chat and the old
feelings return. It's good.
It's as wonderful as it ever was.
It's now. But cold

so snow and ice in the shadows.
A winter walk along the cliffs.
It's all imaginary.
I'm in a city hotel on the other side
and you're somewhere tropical
if I've got the spelling right
(long before fax or email).

Imagine the razorbills in their nests now.
Or was that last summer, or the one before that?
Far below, the swell rises and slaps
against the rock.
No sunlight on those shells.

Snow in the sea spray
the way waves continue to crash
in the darkest dark of midwinter.

No lights out to sea.
The wind. The cold. The wet.
Your voice somewhere

ANDREW SCLATER

Three Sea Poems

Clear Night Black Water

a star

astir

astern

Land Lure

is

island

land

―――――――

sand

sand and

strand

―――――――

sure

unsure

shore

Sma Sea

whit whaup

wi cloopie neb

creckin partanes

willnae strunt the ebb

mang chuckie-stanes

wioot a jaup?

Glossary

chuckie-stanes	pebbles
cloopie	walking stick with curved handle
creckin	cracking
ebb	foreshore
jaup	splash
neb	beak
partanes	crabs
strunt	strut
whaup	curlew

George Shaw [Steel Enclosure]

Stand here beside me on 3 by 2 pavement slabs. There are glass fragments. The levels are not level along the edges. Seams are mossed. Stand at the redbrick wall, hard cement pointed: a rectangular upright to left is a panel that is sullied by a screw. In this same panel we have, to right, the locked door with broken handle and keyless slot. This no-way entry/exit is signed Caution Anti-Vandal Paint In Use. Exclamation. Mark, then, to left of right a panel below a sill with blanked-out window above. And above the above (spanning head of window and door) the horizon is level enough to be dishonest and madden a rectangle taken from dirty white sky, subtending dirty this white heaven and all flaking?

It is written I ♥ DM and also a long oval (inside a wider oval) with some sort idea of eyelashes in two rays around. It is also written LFC, and KING, and HUNT, and WHO'S THAT, and BY POD. It is also here I would build Jerusalem in Coventry's fair and pleasant land along the left side, in the falling shaft of light, indeed, of the structure.

Here is a path to an undisclosed destination. I do not doubt it is the only way out of here—after we have counted the 371 bricks—and after the ancient custodian of our lives has drawn the security bolts at the site entrance, some feet behind. Be vigilant with regard to inequalities of level. Beyond the pressed steel of security.

The little girl has picked her doll
from the ruins of her home
"It used to sing"
It used to
A young fighter bleeds
on the ground from the mouth
Thirteen children have been knived
to death
by Government forces.

Coventry steel melts Damascus.

(The 'George Shaw' poem was written in response to Shaw's 2008 enamel painting entitled *Undergrowth*, which is one of his extensive series of views of the Tile Hill Estate in Coventry.)

Between Two Breaths

1

I wanted one of them to come, to shift
the past around. Behind the door

I was all naked. They told stories in their
language, the people outside who exist

mechanically. Yet I have been in the vicinity
since I was a child. I obey, eyes closed.

Am I ill? If I could have a glass of water, drop
everything, skirts and suchlike.

2

The smell of hair in my face all night. Is it yours
this hand writing notes in the dark

in the margins? I've lost you again. In a while
wake me with the other hand while everyone else

is asleep. She closes the book. Now they want her
without her clothes on

walking slowly. The dream hand greets me.
I go into the interior. Why chase a star?

3

So I will leave for Paris, or lie down. In this fair
as big as a city we come to a dormitory

somewhere between the first and fifth floor.
The blood rushes to our faces already

eaten away. Take out the pad of paper, cross
the space to your room. At last here's the floor

still lucid. But there's filth on your face. *Pardon.*
Between two breaths, *elle m'a dit pardon.*

4

In the sadness of the moment, a shadow changes clothes.
Will I have time to change? More and more

I have moved away. I used to feel guilty at night
accosted by an unknown stranger (he pulls me

behind him, going nowhere), but events
have shifted. Now he's quiet with the truth of a cold house.

I have a rendez-vous
elsewhere. The road is made.

5

Someone wakes me with no sound. My love
is atop but this bed is more often than not

still empty. My whole body
has to find a way, but have I ever left the city

in my room? All the ones I let go. On each floor
they are waiting for me. Everything is ready.

I open my fingers. I wait for the morning air. It speaks
of a forgotten touch, a taste, a mouth emptied.

6

I come to my room. The walls grow transparent.
My bed is at the back. Listen for the foetal heart.

A rusty creature, but if it works you'll come out feeling younger
in black and white. The face wanders in reverse,

then trots, then canters, divine and simple,
speaking of lost summers. You are on the other side

of the black water of a street, asking someone who waits
in the rain unmoving if he knows the way.

Replicas

Each goes without a sound to their own house.
When you are old you will stretch out to the last
stranger with the tips of your fingers.
Even now his odd shadow is scudding across

the empty landscape. It's the quickest way
while you still move with uneven steps
and the tap of a stick. There's no one else
on the narrow path between the trees.

But perhaps I've come too far without
declaring myself. Those I cannot see are near me.
Why cry, I wonder. My mother has come to take me,
my face wet from the snow in her mouth.

I tell you this while I'm still here with you, where I lie
as if there *were* two of us. Your footsteps grow fainter.
The words you hear are not mine. It's night.
I have no weapon, but still you keep your distance.

Return to the Pleasure Beach

all night the harvester's out
bright lights & machinery
for lifting of the beet

an age-old tradition
vanished into shadowplay
unhurried tranquillity
turbulence & unrest
the earliest
                known setting
of the mass for the dead

what can I do
with a single note? sparse
yearning lines
                a piano
grows in a year from timber planks
to its own unique voice

an illicit affair in a small town
grainy & unfinished
polyphonic twists
stark power
raw beauty
a lookout tower
over the uncertain shore
explorations
of sound in space

a ruined boat
half buried in the fen
pitched headlong into intoxicating
colours
 lunar

shimmerings
        pungent ideas
blowing the dust off
forward propulsion

shifting coastline
Martello towers
& a stump
of old tree, roots
fatally steeped in brine

the harpsichord
  breaks
the shackles of convention
genial warmth with echoes
of klezmer & jazz
lustrous viola

sweet stinky cargo
hauled on the reach
redundancies of toilage in the silt
sluice seepages meander deeply etched
to the edge of the mud

a walk among saints
in moated grounds, a tenacious
coastal village
                fishing
& smuggling succeeded
50 years ago
                by the Magnox reactor
drawing in seawater as
an abundant coolant
                        a meditation
on light, energy, the collapse of time
our ambitious
                methods of survival

the Spitfire pilot is also its rescuer
salvaged engine crafted new
by each carefully engineered
turn of the lathe, screw
& turbine, Merlin torque & marque

maquette precision, oiled
to an exact approximation of wear
smell, note & rhythm redolent
of a youth before ours

new footage of the first performance
gesture & structure shaped
with meticulous
fingerwork at Harvard
gothic architecture of the cathedral
nave, sea-going
barque on inland waters

conjuring the last judgement
with the ghost of Bartók
complex minimalism
rhythmic mouse-clicks amplified
to dance & burlesque

precise routes plotted
between
    eastern Europe
& the cafés of Buenos Aires
half the world's population
of grey seals is found
around British coasts

waders at the water's margin
turnstone redshank curlew dunlin
colours mutable with the day's changing mood
somewhere a gull or crow
surprised from its meal
godwit squadrons slice the cooling air

humidity is a key requirement
holes may be chiselled
to a depth of four inches
(the cimbalom anchors
pungent bagatelles
to the heritage of Benny Goodman)
both sexes can drum
trunks & branches
continuing
              until late June

adults feed mainly on cuckooflower
betony, fleabane & buttercup
in complicated sleep
a rusting wing
among scorched nettles

the turnip pile's gone
these ten years

Knee's Interior

In bloom, to prise the shrub of dates jawbone open
and witness the pink interior, these are desires in terracotta
pamphlets about Christmas time, though I'm not sure
the workers' comp case was up by that stage.
A howler, the toast to departmental improvements,
the plaque on the walls, terra firma teased out
as vox populi. I'm not sure the want became the need by this
stage, but copious amounts of acid tea and weltering surf,
and Kris Hemensley's citations of Jurassic coast finitely friable,
all dust. And yet darts my son's lover from the granny flat
upwards and over, knocking apples from the fence line arbour;

Fitzroy is steadfastly cruel to us all. Especially the meridian
rose petals and heady camellias. The false welcome
of dawn blenches the blithe throat, leaves for dead real estate
self fashioning, though you might hear rat bones
in the hinges of the occupied district.
How fascinating, the impossible trill between the 'd'
and the 'l' in middle. Just try and roll your *Arabian Nights*
with that, censor incensed indefinitely anyhow by presentation
in our serious quarters, by presentation of our serious quarters.

Especially desirable, the needs of Christmas. How much flatter might
Australia be. Yanchep, dunes nearby. Every car top treading water is
        a soapbox,
if you ask me, and what stones in its throat.
How might the Datsun have sucked a river stone
compared with the Mazda run aground. Your mother is setting
mousetraps interminably. The knee scars in secret pinkly.

Cryptomeria

Far more cryptomnesia these days, may it
be born then in the chrysalis
of remembrances, the good forgetting forgotten
running his hands through Akita fur

of acres of shivering fibrillating vice figures
of the iodine-poisoned anodised, glade lain in a country
of cryptomeria.

Wades an Ugly Head

A somniation, that fish water, and fuse to torpor's
Robert Mitchum at dusk with his mitts knitted

to the designs of early cretonne. But aren't they just delicious
when the estate has them in lagniappes at the Guild.

Our second honeymoon. O the wafts of sulphur in 1917
that the Welsh collier was paid to call home, and is, home,

the whistling in tongues the stranger understands, tea
with hot water Alzheimer's. She swoons in the calypso air.

Bayou tasks narrow forebodement to the foreseeable and blithe
horizon countermand, rivers of wheat, and the interstitials of corn

that town reaps. Canola is new, thus new business, sung
of a narrow brogue made mythic by its obscurity at the trickle coastline

of the unprehistoric, a limestone best known to Sunday sightseeing
and the new ballast buttress break, what they advertise as 'the
            invalid tour'.

The tolls to tolling new season, design of early tresses tried by hands
too thick for feline hygiene. No swung pig to Kyneton,

no heavy balls to Manjimup, no blood letting on New Cuba.

Cuba sets sail for employment, employment condescends to the
       febrile fit
unemployment that jags the shatter at high rise Melbourne Unity,

seethes the heady germinating club hairs the stirring spoon secret
       of the club
Marcus Clarke; the febrile fit in May. May. May is seeing the prospects

of your final hour
in another's self-portrait
that resembles you.

No One

In Western Australia, the desire to come to know
the no one develops as the xanthorrea
incision lodes. The Zigzag was a railroad is a trek
into the east. Find pink orchids and other invisibles.
Knowing no one, the known washes its hair
in the weir the day it overflows.

Today, we can call it Mundaring, the weir.
Today, you wash your hair. Tomorrow,

you begin the walk again. The wattle cones
are torches are club fists. Thump the one known
with the club fist torch of the wattle until
it perishes the unknown. The weir has lost its body,
is yet still there, kangaroo scat on the breeze
like a public toilet on the Champs-Élysées,
says Marcel, though not to me, says the hunted haunted
West Australia now a car park.
That's what the old folk say. They replaced our town
with a municipal rust cloud of no one.

YVES BONNEFOY

TRANSLATED FROM FRENCH BY
IAN BRINTON & MICHAEL GRANT

Here and Now

Here and now, in the bright place. It is no longer dawn,
But instead the full day of desires that can be spoken.
From the chanting mirage in your dream all that is left
Is this sparkling of stones to come.

Here and now, until evening. The rose of shadows
Will shift across the walls. The rose of hours
Will silently drop its petals. The bright flagstones
Will dictate as is their wont these steps in love with daylight.

Here, and always now. Stone upon stone
Builds the land told of by the memory.
The sound of simple fruits falling scarcely
Fires up in you that healing time again.

(from *Hier régnant désert*, 1958)

The magnet, you said

The magnet, you said, of our lamp and of the leaves,
These hosts of our evenings.
They haul their boats up to us over the flagstones,
Knowing of our desire for the eternal.

Perfect night in the sky cries out its fire,
And they come with an un-shadowed step, to wake us,
Their word begins at the trembling of our voices.

The step of the stars measures the tiled earth of this night,
Mingling with so many fires mankind's own darkness.

(from *Pierre écrite*, 1965)

Tree and Lamp

Throughout the summer the tree grows old inside the tree.
The bird breaks clear of the bird's song and escapes. The red of the
      robe
Flames up, and disperses
Far off, in the sky, the cortege of an ancient sorrow.

O fragile country
Like the flame of a lamp one carries,
Sleep being near the sap of the world,
Simple that pulsing of the divided soul.

You too you love the moment when the lamp's light
Is drained, and dreams in the day.
You know the wound healed in the dark of your heart,
The boat falling again to shore.

(from Pierre écrite, 1965)

Mercurial Motion

There will be no other opportunity. I remove my shoes. A loincloth,
otherwise naked; I sit down. The scroll spread out on the
broad beamed floor is double sized. Kao Chi. From dawn
to midday the mendicant of Green Mountain hums his
poems, has forgotten to eat (ate nothing). Kao Chi, a
beggar; the hermit chanting softly, a mendicant. The third
bowl (a rag?) emptied between my legs, my right hand feels
along the floor, with the fine-haired brush, china ink the
colour of crow feathers, I add a dazzling brightness (I think
of it as inward): everything is ready.

The cat, porcelain white, sea blue mirage, perches frisky on the
windowsill (marked with scratches where it leans out).
Mount Chun, Jade City beyond, a single path, I have no
need now to consult Kao Chi, the man of Green Mountain,
the venerable old Magician. To make the ascent. A brown
robe, coarse flax (dyed, embers). I trust, I trust in the road,
the height, Jade city itself beyond the hillside. The hillside
(I chant softly) the hillside. One word (I chant) as good as
another (neither now nor later is *that* true). I keep some
alms in the only pocket in my robe. My cap, serge; the
sandals, esparto; the walking stick, elder.

Silent. Everything in effect is ready, I contemplate the scroll spread
out on the floor. Kao Chi does not appear. I see that
nothing is grafted onto the paper: I will get no other
opportunity (let's say). To leave, now. The body an elegant
shack; an easy come, easy go hovel. The opportunity
(foreseen perhaps in advance) could permit me once and for
all to take my leave into the distances (of the scroll?) to
return there, dawn, full stop: to leave the (double sized)
scroll stretched out on the wide boards of a pear-wood floor
(will this be possible?): to leave? Not to write, no, not to
write. A juicy bartlett pear in my mouth, to ooze yellow, to

see a few drops trickle from my lips onto the scroll: three stains, finally.

To stand there looking at a pair of kingfishers take flight, on the scroll the intention hovering over my hand which this time did not inscribe the paired presence of the (double) bird genderless direction letters dissolving: two points, and I turn around. A few stains, the diagonal shadow, and I leave: perhaps I have reached the extreme edge (of the paper) the categorical distances from whose jaws Kao Chi descends from a palanquin, gives me an unfoldable bundle of parchment sheets (a living ream of ideograms) and (with a hand I recognise as quite other than my own hand) I give him a broom (a rocking movement, Kao Chi, a rocking back and forth of shadows) I don't know if of dry laurel branches or of broom.

Mercurial Motion

This happened to me in the time of the Three Kingdoms.

I enter and find myself standing on a sphere of esparto grass, I who walked barefoot see that I am wearing sandals of esparto (the mind that, when I entered, was full of the reeds and bulrushes of the riverbank is emptied): I see that my feet in shadow, the sandals removed, have transformed (into esparto).

For the first time I fear rain, unapproachable mother of trans-formations: I am standing on a sphere of esparto grass, this happened without a doubt in the Tang period. It rains. A bird sings. The sound of the waterclock grows in my ears (more than anything in the left ear). A mechanical bird repeats its tune, it never rusts (mechanisms endure) (something to be thankful for): I bend down to take off the (muddied) sandals, sap circulates in the opposite direction to the hands of the (digital) wall clock (a luminous sphere) belly and extremities

(face and for sure likewise my back) of (parched) esparto
(don't let the water wet them, don't let the water wet them):
the year 2004, only my right hand (suspended) remains
flesh, I am on the point of knowing what troubles it, I see
(and with time, and with systematic practice everything
becomes natural) the hand transform into the drowsiness
of paper where the bird glides (it rains) from waterclock
(Tang period) to wall clock, the hand scatters cherry
blossoms, water of May, and the unvaried constancy of
esparto grass.

The exteriorisation of his places

In my country called Cuba there is a fish called manjuarí.

And the dead of my family return riding the backs of cows they
return to their second place that is my country to die truly
on the tame back of the manatí.

She goes there and, immediately, happily becomes one of the women
of my family: impetuous, touched by an almost carnivorous,
almost still fertile scent, the earth indeed: a few simple palm
leaves a few heavy storms lead in a natural way to the almost
silent conversation among family members: and later the
terraces, whether you live or die south is south spring is
found on the western side Cuba is a nation with a brief north
wind a moderate winter, to it my relations came in their
dispersion in their ongoing dispersion of places three horses
tied to a two-horse cart tall white mirrors whose familiar
figure is the ermine.

In principle, the idea of air the superficial idea of air moving above
what happens eliminates the crude idea of a history: to this
my dead testify.

From one sickness or another after the cycles after the shattered body
(in my country they say *cancanea*, 'feeling really crook'), these
dead don't spread out but sit together: on an island in a

given moment when the earth oxygenated by our worm of perfected earth since it is perfect receives encloses the body of any one of those I love whoever it may be or whoever it was or will be or whoever I will be: I place no importance on death since I love the red earth as I love the leaf of the tobacco fields, the flower that in my country they call guajana, I love the vegetable carbon in the brazier that warmed my ancestors my kin of a migratory air.

One of my relatives died one twenty six of March nineteen eighty six she is vegetable carbon guajana tobacco leaf: fertile on her island.

For her soul a sequence, if there is one.

This pertains to time to the passage of time but the mild fields with their tobacco flowers add a dash of colour to the visible geography or, if they came or arrived from a different geographic place, my people would be talking of the hailstorms that beat against the inclined roofs of houses or the rhomboid cleavers of snow that pound the backs of mares.

What more to say about it: the island in its shape is an island.

We go away or we come back, we're not exactly sure which, it's a lot, all that, why should we change?: the form of an island is tautological in shape like someone who says I was born here here on the back of some word like yagua palm manjuarí I come from the north I am scattered I return to die with or without north since in the absence of any other kind of movement I possess the air's prerogative.

To her memory, I pay respect.

Let's go and set the table, she will serve: fifteen relatives, standing there we notice a large loaf slightly crumbled, androgynous in form, a pan pipe's echoing sounds, fragrance of cinamomo trees.

MARINA TSVETAEVA

TRANSLATED FROM RUSSIAN
BY CHRISTOPHER WHYTE

The Greatcoat

1

A greatcoat for all who are tall and well-built,
a greatcoat for all who gaze into the East...

It must be five or six o'clock. A blue-grey haze. Day breaks.
The drinking bout lasted all night, until the seventh hour.
Demon-like, a greatcoat flaps up high over the bridge.
A woman or a demon? A Dominican's black robe?

A tenor from the opera? A widow's humble shawl?
Hiding a playful intrigue? Someone bracing for the end?
The urge to kiss. A siren wails. Gaga aristocrats
shuffle towards their beds, the stupid destitute towards Mass.

March 8th 1918

2

Epoch of crowned intrigues, epoch
of ruffians and greatcoats, for
crowned heads a Golgotha, epoch
when *philosophes* wrote manuals
for courtesans, and something moved
a fop from the beau monde to give
his life up for the greater good.
Beyond the ocean, Lafayette
flashed his sword of rhetoric.
Duchesses of highest rank
disarmed admirers, following
the heart's dictates, and Rousseau's too,
bathed in seas of childlike lace.

Little girls rolled hoops along
and nuns whispered to uniforms
in Tuileries awash with scent...

Meanwhile the queen, a humming-bird,
wrinkling her forehead, talked
to Cagliostro until day broke.

March 11th 1918

3
Machinations of nocturnal swallows—
greatcoats—heroes fitted out with wings
seeking adventures in a world of snobs.
Greatcoat, looking smart even in tatters,
suitable for heretics, freethinkers,
to camouflage a cherub or a rogue.

Greatcoat more capricious than a fleece,
so prone to going down on bended knee
doing its best to win our trust, but dubious…
The nightwatch horn sounds by the thundering Seine.
Casanova's greatcoat, and Lauzun's,
Marie-Antoinette in cloak and mask.

Look! Demon conjured up from forest depths,
the greatcoat's an enchanter, a whirlwind,
a crow hovering above the piebald flock
of butterflies from a world of poseurs.
Greatcoat colour of dreams, of times gone by,
adorning Cavalier Cagliostro's shoulders.

April 10th 1918

Notes on Contributors

Kate Ashton lives in the north of Scotland. She has work on the *Gallery* area of the Shearsman website as well as in a previous issue.

Linda Black lives in London, and has two collections from Shearsman, *Inventory* (2008) and *Roots* (2011).

Yves Bonnefoy (b. 1923) is considered to be France's finest living poet. Among his many publications are *La longue chaîne de l'ancre* (2008) and *Les Planches courbes* (2001), both from Mercure de France, Paris.

Peter Boyle lives in Sydney. His publications include a translation of José Kozer's *Anima* for Shearsman (2011), and *Museum of Space* (University of Queensland Press, 2004).

Susie Campbell lives in Surrey. This is her first appearance in *Shearsman*.

Geraldine Clarkson has poems in *Tears in the Fence, Smiths Knoll, Brittle Star, Envoi, Orbis, Fuselit*, and online at *Eyewear*.

Claire Crowther has two collections from Shearsman, *Stretch of Closures* (2007) and *The Clockwork Gift* (2009).

Mark Dickinson's first collection will appear from Shearsman in 2013. His work was featured in the anthology *The Ground Aslant* (2011)

Ray DiPalma's work has appeared in a number of issues of *Shearsman*. His most recent publication is *The Ancient Use of Stone* (Seismicity Eds, 2009).

Keri Finlayson lives in Swansea. Shearsman published her first collection, *Rooms,* in 2009.

Mark Goodwin has two full collections from Shearsman, *Else* (2008) and *Back of A Vast* (2010), as well as a chapbook, *Layers of Un*, published in June 2012.

Harry Guest turned 80 in October 2012; *High on the Downs. A Festschrift for Harry Guest* was published by Shearsman to celebrate the event. His *Comparisons & Conversions* was published by Shearsman in 2009, and his Collected Poems, *A Puzzling Harvest*, appeared from Anvil in 2002; the same publisher issued a new collection, *Some Times,* in 2010.

Charles Hadfield lives in Auckland, New Zealand. He has four UK collections, the most recent being *The Nothing We Sink or Swim In*, from Oversteps Press, in 2002.

Lucy Hamilton's first collection, *Stalker,* was published by Shearsman in 2012, and was shortlisted by the 2012 Forward Prize jury for the Felix Dennis Prize for the Best First Collection.

José Kozer is a Cuban poet living in Florida. Shearsman published *Anima* in 2011; a *Selected Poems* is also available from Junction Press, New York.

MARY LEADER is a professor at Purdue University in Indiana. Her third collection, *Beyond the Fire*, was published by Shearsman in 2010.

EDWARD MACKAY lives in London, and has poems in *Stand, Poetry Review, Magma*, as well as a forthcoming chapbook, *A Swarming*, from Salt.

JULIE MACLEAN, from Bristol, is currently based on the Surf Coast, Australia. A manuscript was shortlisted for Salt's Crashaw Prize in 2012.

JAMES MCLAUGHLIN lives in Dumbarton and has two chapbooks, *AEIDO* and *Text 1* from Knives, Forks & Spoons Press, Manchester.

JOHN MATEER, originally from Johannesburg, now lives in Perth, WA. His most recent book is *Southern Barbarians* (Giramondo, Sydney, 2011).

ALICE MILLER lives in New Zealand; poems have appeared or are forthcoming in *The Boston Review, The Iowa Review*, and *Best New Zealand Poems*, and a manuscript was shortlisted for Salt's Crashaw Prize in 2012.

SHARON MORRIS lives in London. *False Spring* was published by Enitharmon, who will issue her second collection before the end of 2012.

SEAN REYNOLDS is a doctoral candidate in the Poetics Program of SUNY Buffalo. He co-edited *Wild Orchids*, an annual journal of criticism, and was co-editor of Jack Spicer's selected translations of *Beowulf*, published in the most recent volume of *Lost & Found*.

PETER ROBINSON's latest collection, *The Returning Sky*, was published by Shearsman in 2012 and was a Poetry Book Society Recommendation. He has also recently edited *Bernard Spencer: Essays on his Poetry & Life* for Shearsman.

ROBERT SAXTON's latest collection, *The China Shop Pictures*, was published by Shearsman in October 2012. His previous collections include *Manganese, Local Honey*, and *Hesiod's Calendar*, all from Carcanet/OxfordPoets.

ANDREW SCLATER is "a drystane dyker motorbiker poet from Edinburgh". He is active on the performance scene in Edinburgh and Newcastle, was shortlisted for the Picador Poetry Prize in 2010, and this year has a New Writers Award from The Scottish Book Trust.

IAN SEED has two collections from Shearsman, *Anonymous Intruder* (2009) and *Shifting Registers* (2011).

AIDAN SEMMENS lives in Suffolk. Shearsman published his first collection, *A Stone Dog*, in 2011. He has edited an anthology of poetry from Suffolk, which Shearsman will publish in 2013.

SIMON SMITH has several books from Salt, most recently *London Bridge* (2010), and his translations of Catullus will be published by Carcanet in 2013. He teaches at the University of Kent.

MARINA TSVETAEVA (1892–1941) was one the greatest Russian poets of the 20th century.

CRISTINA VITI is an Italian poet and translator living in London. She has published translations of Valeria Fraccari and Dino Campana into English and of Stephen Watts into Italian. Her translation of Elsa Morante appeared in a previous issue.

COREY WAKELING lives in Melbourne. He has work in *Jacket2, Cordite, Southerly, Geek Mook, Handsome Journal, foam:e, Overland* and *Best Australian Poems 2011*. His chapbook, *Gargantuan Terrier, Buggy or Dinghy*, appeared with Vagabond Press this year.

G.C. WALDREP's fourth collection, *Your Father on the Train of Ghosts*— with the poet John Gallaher—appeared in 2011 from BOA Editions.

CHRISTOPHER WHYTE writes in both Gaelic and English, and translates into both Gaelic and English. A volume of his Tsvetaeva translations, *Moscow in the Plague Year*, will appear from Archipelago.

Recent titles from Shearsman Books

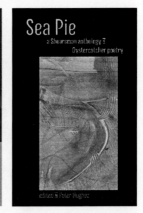

Lightning Source UK Ltd.
Milton Keynes UK
UKOW040415270912

199703UK00001B/15/P